LAKES AND PONDS

A Buddy Book
by
Fran Howard

ABDO
Publishing Company

VISIT US AT

www.abdopublishing.com

Published by ABDO Publishing Company, 4940 Viking Drive, Edina, Minnesota 55435.

Copyright © 2007 by Abdo Consulting Group, Inc. International copyrights reserved in all countries. No part of this book may be reproduced in any form without written permission from the publisher. Buddy Books™ is a trademark and logo of ABDO Publishing Company.

Printed in the United States.

Edited by: Sarah Tieck
Contributing Editor: Michael P. Goecke
Graphic Design: Brady Wise
Image Research: Deb Coldiron, Maria Hosley, Heather Sagisser, Brady Wise
Photographs: Corbis, photos.com

Library of Congress Cataloging-in-Publication Data

Howard, Fran, 1953-
  Lakes and ponds / Fran Howard.
    p. cm. — (Habitats)
  Includes bibliographical references and index.
  ISBN 1-59679-779-7 (10 digit ISBN)
  ISBN 978-1-59679-779-6 (13 digit ISBN)
    1. Lakes—Juvenile literature. 2. Ponds—Juvenile literature. I. Title. II. Series:
Habitats (Edina, Minn.)

QH98.H69 2006
577.63—dc22

                                                    2005031600

TABLE OF CONTENTS

WHAT ARE LAKES AND PONDS?

Lakes and ponds are bodies of water. Lakes are bigger and deeper than ponds. Ponds are small and shallow.

Lakes get their water from **springs**, streams, and rivers. Ponds get much of their water from rainfall.

Lakes and ponds are types of habitats. Habitats are the places where plants and animals find food, water, and places to live. Different plants and animals live in different habitats.

There are a lot of plants and animals that live in and by lakes and ponds.

A goose and its babies near water.

Where Are Lakes and Ponds Found?

Lakes and ponds are found all over the world. They can be found in grasslands, forests, and mountains. Some deserts even have lakes.

The five Great Lakes are in the United States. They are some of the world's biggest lakes. The Great Lakes contain almost one-fifth of the world's **freshwater**.

Lake Ontario

Lake Erie

Lake Huron

The Great Lakes

Lake Superior

Lake Michigan

PLANTS OF LAKES AND PONDS

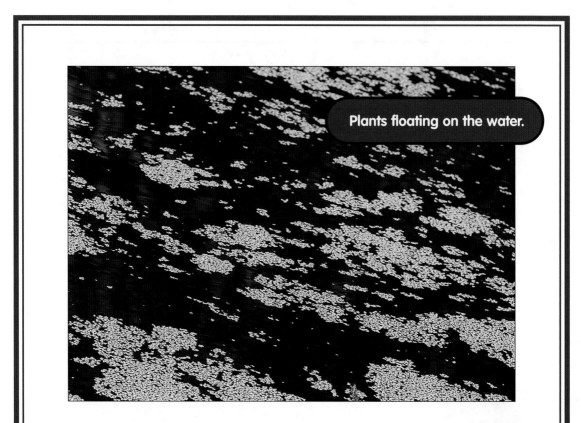

Plants floating on the water.

Some plants float, such as duckweed.
Ducks eat the floating duckweed.

A duck

Most plants of lakes and ponds grow near the shore. The shore is the area where the water meets the land. Water lilies grow close to the shore.

A view of a lake shore.

Water lilies grow in both ponds and lakes. Water lilies need sunshine.

Water lilies have flowers. The flowers come in many colors. Some water lilies bloom at night. Others bloom during the day.

Some water lilies are yellow.
Others are pink or white.

Few plants live in the deep water of a lake. Deep water is too cold and dark for most plants to grow.

Sunlight helps plants to grow on the bottom of a pond. This is because a pond is shallow.

A lot of plants live near the shore.

WATER ANIMALS OF LAKES AND PONDS

Many kinds of animals live in ponds and lakes. Some insects live in the water, while other insects live on the pond water. Water striders are insects that live on ponds. They glide across the top of the water. They eat smaller bugs.

A water strider gliding on water.

A mosquito

Other insects lay eggs in the water. Mosquitoes lay their eggs in ponds.

Many kinds of fish live in ponds and lakes. Both little fish and big fish live in ponds and lakes. Some common fish are walleye, bass, and catfish.

A largemouth bass

Land Animals of Lakes and Ponds

African elephants bathe in a pond.

Many kinds of animals live near ponds and lakes. They get food and water from these habitats.

A deer rests on the shore.

Bears are good swimmers.

Frogs live in the water and on the land. Frogs stay close to their ponds. They lay their eggs in the water. In cold places, frogs bury themselves in mud or sand. They sleep through the cold weather.

Frogs spend time on land and in the water.

Some lily pads are so big that birds can step on them.

Birds live on land. But, some small birds walk on lily pads floating in the water. The birds walk out onto the water to catch bugs.

Canadian geese spend a lot of time in the water.

Turtles live in ponds and lakes. Turtles spend most of the time in the water. They crawl onto rocks or logs to sit in the sun.

A turtle

African hippos

Hippos live in lakes in Africa. Hippos stay in the lake all day. They do this to stay cool. At night, hippos come out to eat plants.

Moose also use ponds and lakes to stay cool. Moose are good swimmers. Sometimes they go underwater to hide from biting flies. In the summer, moose eat water plants from lakes and ponds.

This moose is swimming.

Herons stand in the water and wait for fish to swim by.

Great Blue Herons are water birds. Herons eat fish and frogs. They fish in ponds and lakes. Herons fish by standing very still in the water. When a fish swims by, the bird grabs it with its beak.

This Great Blue Heron is standing on the shore.

WHY ARE LAKE AND POND HABITATS IMPORTANT?

People and animals need lakes and ponds. Lakes and ponds give people fish to eat and water to drink.

People have fun on lakes and ponds. They canoe on lakes and ponds. They water-ski and swim in lakes.

The animals and plants of lakes and ponds need each other. Together they form a **food chain**. Even the smallest plants and animals of ponds and lakes are part of the food chain. Plants and animals of lakes and ponds cannot live without their habitat.

Heron

Frog

Mosquito

LAKES AND PONDS

- In North America, there are five lakes known as the Great Lakes. These are Lake Huron, Lake Ontario, Lake Michigan, Lake Erie, and Lake Superior.

- Sometimes ponds get "scum" on their surfaces. This layer forms because of rotting plants and nutrients in the water.

- Lake Baikal in Russia is the deepest lake in the world. It holds more water than all the Great Lakes combined.

- Even if there is ice covering a pond, the plants and animals in it are alive. Some are even active beneath the surface.

- Some lakes have salt water instead of **freshwater**. The Great Salt Lake in Salt Lake City, Utah, is a salt lake.

- The Caspian Sea is the world's largest lake. It is a salt lake.

IMPORTANT WORDS

food chain the order in which plants and animals feed on each other.

freshwater water that does not contain salt.

spring the point where groundwater rises to the surface.

WEB SITES

Would you like to learn more about **lakes and ponds**? Please visit ABDO Publishing Company on the World Wide Web to find Web site links about **lakes and ponds**. These links are routinely monitored and updated to provide the most current information available.

www.abdopublishing.com

INDEX